AN INSTANT GUIDE TO

TREES

Nearly 200 of the most common
North American trees
described and illustrated in full color

Eleanor Lawrence and Cecilia Fitzsimons

CRESCENT BOOKS
NEW YORK

This 1985 edition published by Crescent Books, distributed by
Outlet Book Company, Inc., a Random House Company,
40 Engelhard Avenue, Avenel, New Jersey 07001.

Random House
New York • Toronto • London • Sydney • Auckland

Manufactured in Malaysia

Library of Congress Cataloging in Publication Data

Lawrence, Eleanor (Eleanor G.)
  An instant guide to trees

  Bibliography: p.
  Includes index.
  1. Trees–Identification.
I. Fitzsimons, Cecilia   II. Title.
QK477.2.14L39   1985   582.16'097   84-24308

ISBN 0-517-46892-1

10 9 8 7 6 5

Contents

Introduction

This is a book for those who enjoy trees but may not have the time or opportunity to make a close study of them, and would appreciate some means of easily identifying a tree that catches their eye along the street, or in the park or countryside. We have selected from the many hundreds of North American trees those species most likely to be encountered in the countryside of the more heavily populated areas of the United States and Canada, and along streets and in parks. Emphasis has been given to trees of the temperate areas of North America (the tropical trees of southern Florida, for example, have not been included, except for a few palms). Some introduced trees, which are widely grown for ornament, have also been included.

For easy identification, the trees in this book have been grouped into sections on the basis of the shape of their leaves (see *Guide to Identification*). Leaves are a useful identifying feature as they are present for much of the year, even on deciduous trees which shed their leaves in winter. As well as foliage, flowers and fruits are illustrated for most of the trees here. Fruits and flowers are often the easiest way of identifying a tree, and so have been emphasized in the descriptions, even though they may be available for only a limited time. It is when flowering in spring or bearing distinctive fruits and seeds in fall that trees most often attract attention.

Because of the wide variety of climate and geography in North America, the area in which a tree is found can be an important clue to its identity. Most trees in the United States fall naturally into two groups, those native to the east, and those to the west of the Rocky Mountains. More detailed information is given in the distribution box for each species (see Fig. 2), which will enable the reader to see at a glance whether they might expect to see that tree wild in their part of North America. It should be noted however, that the tree may not be common, or even present, throughout the whole of that area, and may also be planted elsewhere in parks and gardens in regions with suitable climates, as indicated for many trees. The names of the trees used here are the ones that are now standard and commonly used in reference books; many trees in North America have local names, so although you may be familiar with a tree under another name this does not mean that you have identified it incorrectly.

Lastly, it will do no harm to take a few leaves, or flowers or fruits from a well-established tree growing in the wild, but material should not be taken from trees growing in parks or public gardens. Best of all, take this book with you on your next hike and check out your findings on the spot.

How to use this Book

This book is divided into three basic sections: **Broadleaved trees, Palms and palmlike trees** and **Conifers.** A fourth section, **Lookalikes and other species,** complements the first three. These sections are clearly distinguished by the different colored bands at the top of the page (see Fig. 1).

Fig. 1 Key to tree sections

☐	Broadleaved trees	▨	Palms and palmlike trees
☐	Conifers	☐	Lookalikes and other species

Using the *Guide to Identification* to tree and leaf type overpage, first decide to which of the above sections your tree belongs. The leaf symbols will help you narrow down the field and the information contained on the heading band and in the colored boxes below the illustration of each tree makes a positive identification possible and eliminates confusion. A specimen page is shown in Fig. 2.

PRIMARY FEATURES
Where feasible, you will be able to recognize the tree from the primary characteristics described in the first box, together with the illustration. Sometimes, however, it is only a combination of features that identifies a tree, firstly as belonging to a particular type (e.g. as an oak if it has acorns), and then as a particular species (e.g. as Red Oak by a combination of leaf shape and acorn form). You can be sure you have identified the tree when it has all the characteristics in the first two boxes and is growing in a situation and area consistent with the information in box 3.

FLOWERS AND FRUITS
Flowering and fruiting times are given at the foot of the page, but these are guides only, as they are very variable in different conditions. The fruiting times mostly refer to ripe fruit — immature fruit may be visible on the tree for several months previously and be a useful guide to identification, if allowance is made for differences in size and color. "Fruits" here refers to all types of seeds and their containing structures, not just to the familiar edible fleshy fruits.

The third box is a general guide to where the tree is most likely to be found. For the purposes of this book the dividing line between the

5

eastern and western regions is taken as the eastward edge of the Rocky Mountains. In practice, most typical eastern trees do not reach far into the Great Plains. Further north a number of common trees (e.g. birches and spruces) range across the continent.

In this book NE US includes the area bounded by North Dakota to Maine, south to Maryland and west to Kansas; SE US includes the remaining eastern states with the exception of the Florida peninsula. (Where trees range naturally farther south than northern Florida, this is specifically mentioned.) The majority of the western trees featured in this book come from the coastal belt running from British Columbia through Oregon, Washington State and California. (Other general abbreviations used are: C, central; N, north or northern; S, south or southern; E, east or eastern; W, west or western; CE, central eastern, etc.).

AVOIDING CONFUSION
The fourth box on each page gives the names of some of the commoner trees with which the featured species might be confused, and also some related trees that occur in other areas. Those "lookalikes" printed in heavy type are illustrated, either in full in the main section, or in the *Lookalikes and Other Species* section; those printed in ordinary type are not illustrated. It is important to note that not all the related species have been mentioned, some of which may be common in a particular locality.

Another point to remember is that trees grow slowly, so treat the size indication with caution. In general small trees are those growing up to 30 feet, medium-sized trees are those from 30-70 feet and large trees are those over 70 feet when fully grown, but just because we have indicated that it is a large tree does not mean that you have identified it wrongly if it is small — it may just be young or growing in unfavorable conditions.

Now you are ready to use this book. It is designed to fit in your pocket, so take it with you on your next walk and don't forget to check your sightings on the check-list provided with the index.

Guide to Identification

BROADLEAVED TREES
Trees with a crown of thin, flat, broad leaves growing on woody branches which spread from one or several woody stems or trunks. These trees bear flowers at certain times of the year. Some carry just one type of easily recognizable flower (e.g. Mountain Ash or the magnolias) but a number have two different sorts, male and female, sometimes even on separate trees. Where a tree bears separate male and female flowers, the male flowers are easily distinguished by

their pollen-bearing stamens, which often give the flowers a fluffy appearance in the mass. Often these flowers are very small and are clustered together in heads, sometimes in the form of the familiar catkins (e.g. willows and oaks). Some flowers lack petals (e.g. elms and ash-trees). Lastly, some flowers are very tiny and inconspicuous, so look carefully. The flowers mostly develop into some kind of dry or juicy fruit. If your tree fits this description, then consult the following subsections:

Trees with simple leaves
In these trees the leaves are entire and undivided and not lobed in any way. Very many trees have leaves of this type and so, to enable you to find your tree more quickly, we have divided the subsection into three groups.

Fig. 2 Specimen page

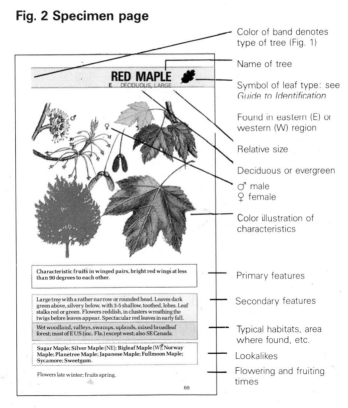

Color of band denotes type of tree (Fig. 1)

Name of tree

Symbol of leaf type: see *Guide to Identification*

Found in eastern (E) or western (W) region

Relative size

Deciduous or evergreen

♂ male
♀ female

Color illustration of characteristics

Primary features

Secondary features

Typical habitats, area where found, etc.

Lookalikes

Flowering and fruiting times

The content shown in the specimen page illustration:

RED MAPLE
E   DECIDUOUS, LARGE

Characteristic fruits in winged pairs, bright red wings at less than 90 degrees to each other.

Large tree with a rather narrow or rounded head. Leaves dark green above, silvery below, with 3-5 shallow, toothed, lobes. Leaf stalks red or green. Flowers reddish, in clusters wreathing the twigs before leaves appear. Spectacular red leaves in early fall.

Wet woodland, valleys, swamps, uplands, mixed broadleaf forest; most of E US (inc. Fla.) except west; also SE Canada.

Sugar Maple; Silver Maple (NE); Bigleaf Maple (W); Norway Maple; Planetree Maple; Japanese Maple; Fullmoon Maple; Sycamore; Sweetgum.

Flowers late winter; fruits spring.

69

Simple leaves without teeth In these trees the edges of the leaves are generally toothless. However, some of the leaves may have a few irregular teeth or the edges may be so finely toothed that it is quite difficult to decide whether they are toothed or not. If in doubt, you should check the beginning of the group of trees with simple leaves and single teeth as well. Some of the leaves in this group have edges that are wavy (see Witch Hazel) or spiny or both. Spines are not the same as teeth (see Holly, for example). If you are unsure whether your leaf has wavy edges or is very shallowly lobed, look in the section on trees with lobed leaves as well.

Simple leaves with single teeth In these trees the leaves have edges which may bear sharp or rounded, fine or coarse teeth. If the leaves of your tree are so finely toothed that you are unsure of their placement, or if some are toothed and some are not, then you should look in the section on trees with simple leaves without teeth as well.

Simple leaves with double teeth In these trees the leaves have quite coarsely toothed edges in which the coarse teeth are also toothed — hence double teeth.

Trees with lobed leaves In these trees the blades of the leaves are divided into lobes, either pairs of lobes along the length of the leaf, as in the White Oak diagram on the left, or into more triangular lobes, as in Sycamore. In none of these leaves do the lobes extend to the base of the leaf or to the central line of the leaf, to divide it into separate leaflets. If you have a leaf that is split right to the base or to the central line, you should look at the next section, on trees with compound leaves.

Trees with compound leaves The blades of these leaves are divided into either a few or many separate leaflets, usually along the length of the leaf as in the Mountain Ash diagram on the left, but sometimes the leaflets all grow from one point at the top of the leafstalk, as in the Buckeye. Some compound leaves are further subdivided (e.g. Kentucky Coffee tree).

PALMS AND PALM-LIKE TREES

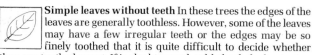

Trees in which the trunks are formed from old leaf-bases: they are not real, woody trunks at all. The leaves grow in a dense crown from the tops of the trunks and may be simple, fan-shaped or finely divided compound leaves. If your tree fits this description you can turn directly to the featured plants of this section.

CONIFERS

Trees with a regular appearance and very many small, either needle-like or scale-like leaves growing from woody branches spreading from a single woody trunk. These trees bear small separate male and female "flowers" like miniature cones. The female flowers develop into mature woody cones which contain the seeds, or in a few species, into seed-bearing "berries." If your tree fits this description, then consult the following subsections:

 Trees with needle-like leaves In these trees the leaves are like needles. They may grow in rows or spirals along the branches, or they may grow in clusters (see Tamarack) or in bundles (see the pines).

 Trees with scale-like leaves In these trees the leaves are small and scale-like and clothe the branches so closely that the twigs often look green and feathery.

Glossary of Terms

Bract A modified leaf which may resemble a petal (see Flowering Dogwood) or be green (see Green Ash), in all cases it has a flower (or flowers) arising at its base, and may remain on the plant with the fruit.

Capsule A dry fruit which splits open to release the seeds.

Deciduous A deciduous tree is one which loses its leaves in winter.

Evergreen An evergreen tree is one which bears leaves throughout the year.

Fruits These contain the seeds. They may be dry or juicy, brown or brightly colored, prickly or smooth etc.

Opposite leaves Leaves growing in pairs on opposite sides of a stem or twig. This arrangement is relatively uncommon when compared with the arrangement known as "alternate leaves" in which the leaves grow alternately from each side of the twig.

Shoot A new young growth.

Stamens The pollen-producing structures of a flower.

Sucker A shoot growing directly from the roots of a tree or shrub; it may be growing some distance from the parent plant and will eventually form a new tree.

♂

Fruits are acorns. Leaves narrow, unlobed, tipped with a small bristle; smooth or slightly hairy beneath, bright green and slightly shiny above.

Large rounded tree with slender twigs. Acorns around ½in long, brown, almost round, in shallow cups. Leaves turn golden in the fall. Male flowers in thin hanging catkins, females small, at the base of the leaves.

Lowlands; SE US. Also planted as a street and shade tree.

Shingle Oak (CE US); **Live Oak** (SE); **California Live Oak** (Calif. coast and foothills); **Canyon Live Oak** (Coast Ranges & Sierra Nevada to S Calif.); **Laurel Oak** (SSE).

Flowers spring; acorns ripen in fall of their second year.

10

Fruits are acorns. Leaves unlobed, leathery, with a rounded tip, edges often rolled under, shiny dark green above, very hairy gray beneath, occasionally with a few teeth.

Medium-sized very broad tree with a short trunk. Acorns around ¾in long, narrow, green becoming very dark brown in paler cups, on long stalks. Flowers similar to those of other oaks.

Sandy soils, dunes; SSE US (including Florida) and northwards along the coast. Also planted as a shade tree.

Willow Oak; Laurel Oak; Shingle Oak; California Live Oak (Calif. coast and foothills); **Canyon Live Oak** (Coast Ranges and Sierra Nevada to S California).

Flowers spring; acorns ripen in the fall of their first year.

Large white or pink "flowers" 3-4in across, made up of 4 large bracts surrounding a mass of tiny yellow-green true flowers, appearing before the leaves.

Small spreading tree. Fruits are oval, shiny red berries in tight clusters at the end of a long stalk, the mealy, bitter flesh enclosing 1 or 2 seeds. Leaves turn bright red in the fall.

Roadsides, old fields, broadleaf forest; most of E US. Cultivated varieties widely grown as ornamentals.

Pacific Dogwood (west coast).

Flowers early spring; fruits in fall.

12

Large, tulip-shaped flowers, with white or pink petals stained purple at the base, borne singly at the tips of the shoots before the leaves appear, opening out widely.

A small spreading tree. Leaves dull green above, covered with fine hairs below. Upright, conelike, fruiting head made up of many small fruits which split to reveal red seeds.

Widely planted in gardens and parks in temperate regions of the US.

Bigleaf Magnolia; Sweetbay; Cucumber Tree; Southern Magnolia.

Flowers early spring; fruits in fall.

Large, bowl-shaped, very fragrant flowers, 6-8in across, with 3 white sepals and at least 6 white petals.

Medium-sized evergreen tree. Leaves shiny bright green above, reddish and hairy beneath, thick and leathery. Large oblong fruiting heads made up of many small fruits that split open to reveal red seeds.

Mixed broadleaf woods in valleys and low uplands; SE US to C Fla. Widely grown in warmer regions; wall shrub further north.

Sweetbay; Saucer Magnolia; Bigleaf Magnolia; Cucumber Tree; Rhododendron; Camellia.

Flowers late spring and summer; fruit early fall.

14

CALIFORNIA BAY LAUREL
W   EVERGREEN, MEDIUM

Rounded clusters of pale yellow flowers at base of leaves at the ends of the twigs in late winter or early spring.

Medium-sized evergreen tree (sometimes a shrub). Leaves thick and leathery, aromatic when crushed, shiny dark green above, with a noticeable network of veins below. Fruit is a greenish to purple berry, around ¾in long.

Canyons and valleys, mixed forest; from SW Oregon to S California in mountains. Also planted as an ornamental.

None.

Flowers late winter, early spring; fruits late fall.

Fruits are red berries in clusters at base of leaves and along twigs; only female trees bear berries.

Small to medium-sized tree, with a narrow, rounded head. Leaves dull green above, yellow-green beneath, with sharp spiny tips and edges Flowers small, white, in clusters along twig, male and female on separate trees.

Lowlands, floodplains, broadleaf forest; SE US to C Florida. Planted as an ornamental; varieties with variegated leaves.

English Holly has shiny dark green leaves and more berries to the cluster; Yaupon (SSE) has evergreen leaves with fine wavy teeth; Possumhaw (SE) has deciduous wavy-toothed leaves.

Flowers spring; berries in fall.

16

Fruits are lemons, oranges (sweet and sour), grapefruits, limes, tangerines etc., all with a thick, distinctively scented rind and sweet or sour juicy flesh.

Small trees and bushes. Leaves leathery, shiny above. Twigs often thorny (lemons, sour orange, grapefruit). Flowers white, with 5 petals, sweetly scented.

Planted across US, in south.

Sour Orange leaves have many tiny teeth and flowers are in clusters.

Flowers spring; fruits in fall.

17

MADRONE
EVERGREEN, MEDIUM   **W**

Flowers small, white tinged with pink, bell-shaped, in upright clusters at the ends of the twigs.

Medium-sized tree with a rounded crown. Branches have reddish peeling bark. Leaves wide, leathery, shiny dark green above. Berries in large clusters, round, warty, red when ripe.

Uplands, canyons, forests; west coast from S California to SW Canada.

None.

Flowers early spring; fruits in fall.

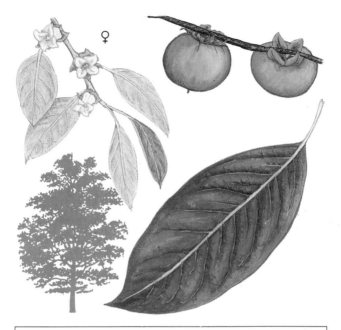

Fruit round, orange to purple brown, stalkless, soft and juicy when ripe, astringent when not ripe; four-lobed woody sepals persist on the fruit.

Small or medium-sized tree. Female flowers white, sweetly scented, bell-shaped, almost stalkless, borne singly at the base of the leaves. Males similar, in clusters of 2 or 3, on separate trees.

Many habitats, roadsides, old fields, forest clearings; E US south from Connecticut (including Florida), except in west.

Introduced species of persimmons with larger fuit are cultivated; Texas Persimmon has black fruit that stains hands and mouth.

Flowers spring; fruits in fall, edible after frosts.

Green-brown fruit, cylindrical, slightly curved, 3-5in long; soft pulp has a custard flavor.

Shrub or small tree. Flowers have 3 prominent, triangular, green, brown or purple outer petals. Crushed leaves have an unpleasant odor.

Broadleaf forest; E US except north, west and extreme south.

None.

Flowers early spring; fruits in fall.

Flowers bright yellow, with thread-like petals, in clusters along bare branches in late fall and winter.

Shrub or small tree. Light brown fruits partly 4-lobed, splitting open to eject 2 black shiny seeds when ripe.

Broadleaf forest; NE and SE US to C Florida. Also planted as an ornamental.

European Alder (when not in flower); Springtime Witch Hazel (SE US) carries similar flowers in spring.

Flowers fall or winter; fruits in fall.

BLACK TUPELO
DECIDUOUS, LARGE **E**

Black berries with a whitish bloom in small clusters on a long
stalk, flesh sour or bitter, enclosing a single ridged stone.

A large tree. Male flowers greenish, tiny, in heads on long stalks
at the base of the leaves; female flowers in clusters of 2-6 on
separate trees. Glossy green leaves turn bright red in fall.

Broadleaf and pine forests, in swamps in SE; E US except
southwest and northwest.

Water Tupelo, fruits borne singly, grows in water in SE swamps;
the red fruits of the small, shrubby Ogeechee Tupelo (N Florida)
are used like limes in preserves and for juice.

Flowers early spring; fruits in fall.

Large, round, heavy, yellow-green fruit with a finely wrinkled surface.

A medium-sized tree with spiny twigs. Leaves shiny dark green above, paler below. Flowers small, green, in small round clusters, male and female on separate trees.

Original range uncertain; now widely planted and naturalized in E & NW US.

None.

Flowers early spring; fruits in fall.

Small white flowers crowded into round heads on upright stalks.

A small tree or shrub with crooked branches. Leaves shiny above, becoming nearly evergreen in the south. Round fruiting heads are made up of many small brown seeds.

By streams and lakes; E US (including Fla.) and SE Canada; also Arizona and California.

None.

Flowers late spring thru summer; fruits in fall.

Masses of delicate, white, sweetly-scented flowers, in hanging clusters, appearing with the new leaves.

A small shrubby tree. Shiny green leaves on purple stalks turn yellow in the fall. Fruits are blue-black long-stalked berries in hanging clusters.

Valleys, broadleaf forest; SE & SNE US.

None.

Flowers late spring; fruits in fall.

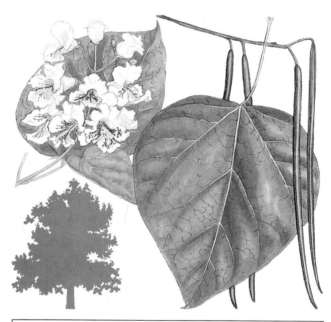

Showy white flowers borne in wide upright spikes;
individual flowers with orange blotches and stripes and
purple spots inside.

A medium-sized spreading tree with a short trunk. Leaves very
large (to 10in long), dull green above, downy below, in opposite
pairs or whorls of 3. Fruits are long, thin, green pods, round in
section, turning brown when ripe and splitting into 2.

Native to small area of SE US; now planted widely as an
ornamental and shade tree in east and west, and naturalized.

Paulownia.

Flowers late spring; fruits in fall.

Flowers bright pink, pea-like, in clusters, growing directly out of larger branches as well as from smaller twigs, appearing before the leaves.

Small spreading tree. Leaves heart-shaped, dull green above, paler below, turning yellow in the fall. Fruits are flat pods, splitting when ripe to release the flat brown seeds like tiny beans.

Valleys, broadleaf forest; most of E US (to C Fla.) except far W and N. Planted as an ornamental, also in western states.

California Redbud, from the hills and canyons of California, Arizona and Utah, has almost round leaves and similar flowers.

Flowers early spring; fruits late fall, early winter.

27

Variety illustrated is Bluegum Eucalyptus

Two kinds of leaves on the same tree — juvenile leaves, often blue and clasping the stem, sometimes green with short stalks; adult leaves long, drooping, lance-shaped.

Medium-sized or large trees, often graceful. Flowers in fluffy white clusters at the base of the leaves. Flower buds form on the tree up to a year before they open.

Naturalized in California; grown as an ornamental in parks and gardens in warmer regions.

A large group of trees native mostly to Australia; many are grown in America. **Red Iron-bark Eucalyptus.**

Flowers open in late summer.

Leaves very small, scale-like, sheathing the twigs, giving the plant a feathery appearance.

A shrub or small tree with very slender, graceful branches. Flowers pink or white in many dense clusters along the branches.

Introduced as an ornamental; naturalized along waterways; W & SW US.

None.

Flowers late spring, summer; fruit summer.

29

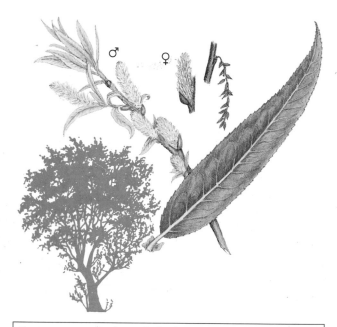

Leaves narrow, finely toothed, often slightly curved to one side, green both sides, shiny above, paler below; leaf-stalks hairy

The largest of the many narrow-leaved willows found across N America. Flowers massed into narrow catkins, appearing with the leaves. Male catkins yellow, 1-2in long, females green, on separate trees, later white and fluffy with seed.

Wet places, often by streams and lakes; widespread in E, also W Tex. west to Calif. Willows as a group are found all over N Am.

Some other tree willows: **White Willow** (E); Pacific Willow (Pacific States & W Canada); Peachleaf Willow (northern plains) leaves are white beneath; Crack Willow (NE) twigs snap audibly.

Flowers spring; fruits late spring

♀

Characteristic long, weeping branches may touch the ground.

A large tree. Leaves finely-toothed, dark green above, gray-white beneath, with long points. Flowers are green catkins (trees usually female).

Parks and gardens especially near water; planted in eastern and western states.

White Willow.

Flowers spring; fruits late spring or early summer.

31

Silvery, furry male catkins on bare branches, upright, stalkless, yellow with pollen later.

A shrub or small tree. Female catkins on separate trees; they are upright, stalkless, green at first, later white and fluffy with seed. Leaves wavy-toothed, shiny green above, whitish below.

Wet meadows, by streams and lakes, coniferous forests; NE US and through central Canada to E British Columbia.

Bebb Willow is a small tree with similar leaves, small yellow catkins, and often diamond-shaped patterns on its bark. Many other shrubby "broad-leaved" willows grow in N America.

Flowers late winter, early spring; fruits early spring.

Variety illustrated is Garden Plum

Fruit is the plum, sweet or sour, juicy fruit, yellow, red or purple, drooping in small clusters or singly.

Small tree or suckering shrub. Flowers white, with 5 equal petals, in small clusters. Leaves of Garden Plum dull green above, more or less hairy beneath. Wild species of plums often bear thorns.

Many varieties cultivated for their fruit and as ornmentals throughout North America.

Sweet Cherry; Japanese Cherries; Apple; Pear; Sweet Crab Apple.

Flowers early spring; fruits summer.

Flowers white, in long, dense, slightly drooping spikes;
crushed leaves and bark have a distinctive smell of cherries.

Medium-sized tree with an oblong crown. The smooth dark gray
bark splits to expose reddish inner bark. Fruits are strings of
small juicy cherries, dark red turning black, slightly bitter but
edible.

Many places except where particularly wet or dry; most of E US.

Common Chokecherry (N & C US and S & C Canada) has similar
leaves and flowers but dark red or black fruits are very bitter;
Hollyleaf Cherry (SW coastal strip).

Flowers late spring; fruits late summer.

Clusters of 2-6 sweet cherries, at first yellow flushed with red, then dark purple unless eaten by birds first.

A medium-sized tree with red-brown peeling bark marked with horizontal stripes. White flowers in clusters of 2-6 appear with the leaves or just before. Leaves are dull green above and paler beneath, coarsely and sometimes doubly saw-toothed.

Along roadsides and edges of woods in NE US and the Pacific States. Many cultivated varieties grown for their fruit.

Japanese Cherries; Pin Cherry (NE US & Canada); Bitter Cherry, with inedible red or black cherries and larger clusters of flowers, is the common wild cherry of the western states.

Flowers early spring; fruits summer.

Variety illustrated is 'Kanzan'

Flowers large, bright pink, white or light pink, often double or semi-double, in clusters, usually opening just before the leaves.

A large group of medium-sized trees often with spreading or even horizontal branches. Some varieties are very narrow and upright, some have weeping branches. Many have bronze-colored leaves.

Introduced and cultivated varieties planted along streets and in yards throughout temperate N America.

Sweet Cherry; Peach.

Flowers early spring; fruits summer or not produced.

Fruits are small, long-stalked, rather sour, yellow-green apples, in clusters of 3 or 4.

A small tree with a broad open crown. Fragrant flowers are white tinged with pink or all pink, in clusters of 4-6, appearing with the new leaves. Coarsely toothed leaves are sometimes almost 3-lobed.

In forest clearings, by streams; ENE US except far N. Varieties of this and other crab apples grown as ornamentals.

The similar Prairie Crab Apple is common farther W, with sometimes spiny twigs; S Crab Apple (SE) has similar leaves, pink flowers; **Oregon Crab** (Alaska to N Calif.); **Pear; Apple.**

Flowers spring; fruits late summer.

37

Fruits are clusters of round, greenish or dark red berries, developing from large clusters of white flowers.

Small shrubby tree with round spreading crown. Twigs bear many very long thin spines. Leaves spoon-shaped, shiny dark green above.

Valleys, low uplands; most of E US except far N and W, also in SE Canada. Also planted as an ornamental and hedging shrub.

One of many native hawthorns, some of which have lobed leaves, but similar flowers and clusters of (usually) bright red berries; **Washington Thorn.**

Flowers late spring, early summer; fruits late fall.

Fruits are red or purple 4-lobed capsules, splitting open to show seeds with bright red seed coats.

Spreading shrub or small tree. Leaves opposite, finely toothed, turning light yellow in fall. Flowers tiny, dark red or purple, in clusters at base of leaves.

Thickets, forest edges; central E US.

European Spindle, with pale yellow flowers and bright pink fruits, is an escape from cultivation in parts of E US.

Flowers late spring, early summer; fruits in fall.

Clusters of small, star-shaped white flowers, with 5 narrow petals, cover the tree before the leaves appear in spring.

A shrub or small tree. Leaves softly white-haired beneath when young. Fruits are small, purple, edible berries, like small apples, and may be juicy or dry.

In broadleaf forests; most of E US except far west, also SE Canada. Also cultivated as an ornamental.

Several very similar species of serviceberries grow throughout eastern and northwestern N America, including Alaska.

Flowers spring; fruits early summer.

Long sprays of small, cream-colored, narrow mouthed bell-shaped flowers, hanging down on one side of a central stalk.

Medium to large conical tree. Shiny yellow-green leaves are sour to the taste; they turn deep red in fall. Fruits are small capsules standing upright on short stalks along a drooping central stalk, remaining on the tree into winter.

Valleys, uplands, moist, fertile, mixed woodland; SE US.

None.

Flowers summer; fruits in fall.

Fruits are prickly brown burs which split into 4 lobes to reveal shiny brown 3-angled nuts — the beechnuts.

A large spreading tree with smooth gray bark, even on old trees. Leaves dull blue-green above, turning orange and yellow in the fall. Male flowers in pale yellow hanging clusters, females in pairs, reddish green, both appearing with the leaves.

Beechwood forests in E US, also extensively planted for shade and ornament.

European Beech is widely planted in NE US and the Pacific States, various forms with ornamental foliage are grown; **Copper Beech.**

Flowers spring; fruits in fall.

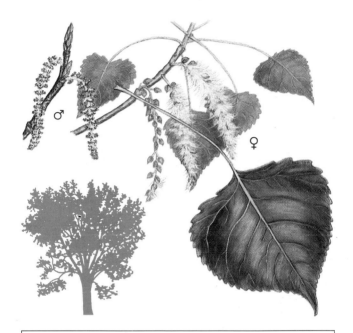

Female catkins produce long (8in) strings of bead-like fruits, green to light brown, which split into 3 or 4 parts to release masses of white cottony seeds.

Large spreading tree. Leaves large, triangular, with coarse curved teeth, shiny green above, turning yellow in fall. Flowers in separate male and female catkins, brownish, male and female catkins on separate trees.

By streams and in valleys, widespread in E US. Cottonwoods as a group are found throughout most of N America.

Black Cottonwood (W N Amer.); **Quaking Aspen; Bigtooth Aspen;** Balsam Poplar and its ornamental form Balm-of-Gilead (NE US thru Canada to Alaska) similar leaves but aromatic buds.

Flowers early spring; fruits spring.

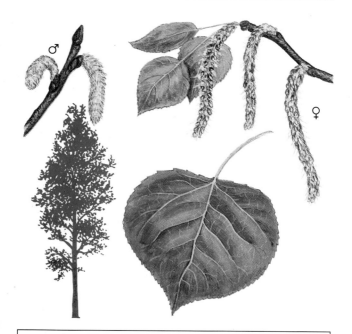

Heart-shaped, finely-toothed leaves with pointed tips, shivering constantly on flattened leaf-stalks.

Medium-sized narrow tree. Male and female catkins brownish, with silvery hairs, on separate trees, before leaves appear. Female catkins produce strings of light green fruits splitting in 2 to release cottony seeds (seed rarely produced in west).

Uplands, mountains; widespread throughout N America from Alaska to NE US & south in western mountains.

Bigtooth Aspen (NE US & SE Canada); **Common Cottonwood.**

Flowers early spring; fruits late spring.

Branches all ascending to give a very characteristic outline to this medium-sized tree.

Trees all male; catkins reddish, not fluffy, appearing before the leaves. Leaves often triangular in outline, leaf-stalks yellow-green in color, flattened.

Widely planted as shelterbelts, screens and as an ornamental throughout most of the US.

Cottonwoods; Aspens.

Flowers early spring; no fruit.

45

Flowers white, tinged with pink, especially in bud, bell-shaped, in hanging clusters of 2-5 on long stalks.

A small tree. Fruits are dark brown, cigar-shaped pods with 4 wings. Leaves turn yellow in fall.

Southern Appalachians, local elsewhere. Also grown elsewhere as an ornamental.

Several local species of silverbell occur in different parts of the SE.

Flowers early spring; fruits late summer to fall.

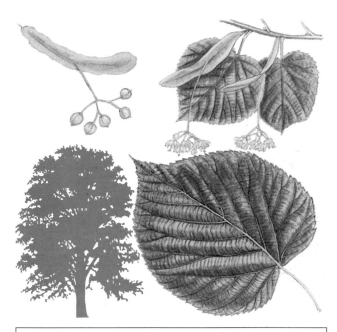

Characteristic flying bracts at first bear small clusters of
fragrant, yellow-white flowers, later clusters of small round
or oval woody nutlets.

Large tree often with 2 or more trunks. Large (3-6in long)
heart-shaped leaves with pointed tips, shiny dark green above,
paler below, almost hairless.

Valleys, uplands, broadleaf forests; NE US and extreme SE
Canada. Also planted as a street and shade tree.

All basswoods and lindens bear similar fruit and flowers;
European Linden has smaller leaves; White Basswood (ECE US)
has leaves coated with white hairs beneath.

Flowers early summer; fruits late summer and fall.

Fruit — the mulberry — is a dense cylindrical cluster of tiny berries, red to dark purple, sweet, juicy and edible when ripe.

Medium-sized tree with a rounded crown. Dull dark green leaves, rough above, are often divided into 2 or 3 lobes. Male and female flowers in separate spikes, both small, on the same tree. Young shoots have a milky sap.

Broadleaf forests; throughout E US (to southern Florida) except far north. Also cultivated for its fruit.

White Mulberry (E & W US); **Paper Mulberry** (SNE & SE US including Florida).

Flowers spring; fruits late spring.

Orange-red to dark purple dry, sweet berries, borne singly on slender stalks.

A medium-sized rounded tree often with "witches brooms." Shiny green leaves with long points are sharply toothed except towards the base. Male and female flowers small, green, on long stalks from the bases of the leaves.

Valleys, upland slopes, broadleaf forests; NE US (except far north) and northern SE US. Also planted.

Sugarberry (SE US); Netleaf Hackberry (SW US) has leaves with a raised network of veins beneath.

Flowers early spring; fruits in fall.

49

Spiny green cups split open to reveal several deep brown shiny edible nuts.

A large tree with wide spreading branches and twisted, furrowed bark. Flowers in catkins, a few green female flowers at the base, yellow male flowers along most of the length of the catkin.

Planted throughout most of the warmer temperate parts of the US.

The similar American Chestnut is now only seen as sprouts from stumps; **Chinkapins;** Golden Chestnut (W coast) has similar spiny fruits but leathery leaves without teeth.

Flowers summer; fruits in fall.

♂

Fruits are acorns, brown, egg-shaped, more than a third
enclosed by a thin cup covered with warty, hairy scales.

Large tree with an open crown. Leaves like those of a chestnut,
with 10-16 blunt teeth on each side. Flowers appear with the
leaves; males, reddish, in thin catkins, females inconspicuous, at
the base of the leaves.

Dry uplands, drier lowland sites, dry woods; eastern half of E
US, except north and south.

Chinkapin Oak (E US, uplands); Swamp Chestnut Oak (SE).

Flowers early spring; acorns ripen in fall of their first year.

Female catkins develop into clusters of small, brown, barrel-shaped, woody "cones," remaining on the tree after shedding seed. These "cones" are typical of all alders.

Medium-sized tree with a narrow head and drooping branches. Leaves oval, dark green above, grayish below. Male catkins yellowish, drooping, 4-6in long, in clusters, appearing before the leaves. Female catkins become green then brown.

By streams, wet soils, lower mountain slopes; Pacific Northwest from SE Alaska to central Calif. Also grown as an ornamental.

European Alder (NE US & SE Can.); White Alder (S. Calif.) has long gold catkins on bare branches in winter. Other shrubby alders are common throughout N America.

Flowers early spring, fruits late summer, remaining on tree.

EUROPEAN WHITE BIRCH

E & W DECIDUOUS, MEDIUM

Graceful, open-crowned tree with white bark, often marked with black, and smaller branches drooping.

Medium-sized tree. Leaves small, triangular, with long points. Male catkins yellow, slender, drooping, females, green, upright, on the same twig. Female catkins produce papery brownish hanging "cones," containing many small 2-winged seeds.

Planted throughout the US as an ornamental. Leaves of ornamental forms often finely divided or lobed.

White-barked birches occur throughout northern N America. **Paper Birch** (E & W); **Gray Birch** (NE US); Yellow Birch (NE) has yellowish bark and an odor of wintergreen from crushed leaves.

Flowers early spring; fruits in fall.

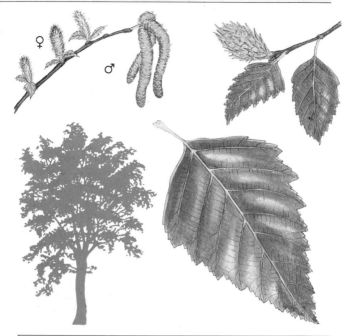

Female catkins mature into brownish, papery, upright
"cones" with many 2-winged hairy seeds.

Medium-sized spreading tree. Bark pinkish-brown or gray,
becoming shaggy with age. Leaves often diamond-shaped, shiny
dark green above, whitish hairs below. Male catkins yellow,
drooping, females green, upright, on the same twig.

By streams, lakes, and in swamps and floodplains. Most of E US
except north and west.

All birches have similar flowers and fruits: Sweet Birch is an
upland tree (NE US) with smooth, shiny, dark brown bark;
Water Birch is a shrubby tree of the mountains of SW & W US.

Flowers early spring; fruits late spring or early summer.

54

AMERICAN ELM

E DECIDUOUS, LARGE

Round, flat, winged fruits with one seed in center have the broad wing deeply notched and a fringe of white hairs around the edge.

Large spreading tree. Small reddish-green flowers on long stalks in clusters along twigs before leaves appear. Dark green leaves, 3-6in long, with unequal bases, are smooth or only slightly rough above.

Valleys, bottomlands; most of E US. Once common, it has now been devasted by Dutch Elm Disease, with other native elms.

All elms have round winged fruits. Slippery Elm (E US) has very rough leaves; Rock Elm (NC US) leaves are shiny and smooth; English Elm has dark red flowers; **Chinese Elm** (Pacific States).

Flowers early spring; fruits early spring.

Fruits of Hornbeam are paired, hairy, greenish nutlets, each cupped in a 3-lobed greenish leafy bract, in loose hanging clusters, later turning brown.

Small shrubby tree with thin, smooth, blue-gray bark. Flowers tiny, appearing before the leaves. Male flowers in catkins, greenish, drooping; female, reddish green flowers in small catkins on same tree.

By streams, broadleaf forests; most of E US except west.

Ironwood or Hophornbeam is a small to medium-sized tree with similar leaves but fruits are cone-like clusters of papery sacs each enclosing a small nutlet (see illus. above); **Beech.**

Flowers early spring; fruits late summer.

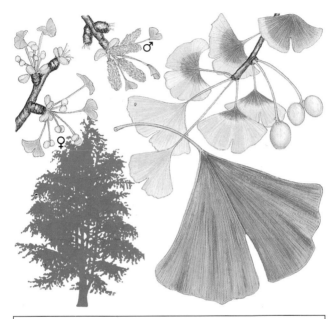

Unique fan-shaped leaves, often divided into 2 lobes; leaves turn bright yellow in the fall.

Medium to large conical tree. Despite its leaves Ginkgo is a very primitive conifer and so does not bear flowers as such. The "fruits," which have an unpleasant odor when ripe, are the female "seeds." Male pollen cones are borne on separate trees.

Planted widely in temperate climates in E US and on the Pacific coast.

None.

"Flowers" early spring; seeds shed in the fall.

Male catkins red and gray-fluffy; female catkins green at first, later fluffy with seed.

Large spreading tree with many suckers. Young shoots and undersides of leaves with bright, white, furry down. Summer leaves of suckers always lobed, other leaves very variable in shape, basically rounded.

Roadsides and edges of fields, naturalized throughout southern Canada and across USA.

None.

Flowers spring; fruits summer.

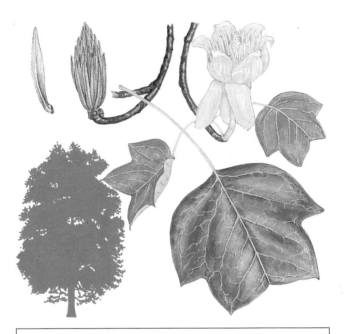

Unusually shaped leaves have flat "cut-off" ends.

Large, tall tree. Upright green and yellow bowl-shaped flowers borne singly at the ends of the twigs. Fruits are distinctive, conical, made up of many narrow-winged seeds.

Valleys, upland slopes; most of the eastern half of E US. Also planted widely as an ornamental.

None.

Flowers spring; fruits in fall.

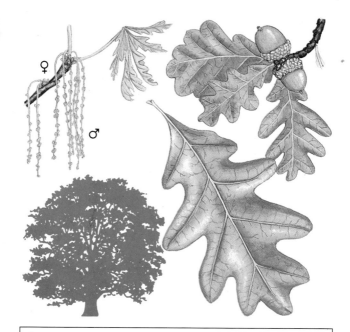

Fruits are acorns, egg-shaped, brown when ripe, in knobby, gray cups covering less than a third of the acorn.

A large broad tree. Leaves with 2-4 pairs of large, narrow, rounded lobes without bristle tips; leaves turn rich orange or brown in the fall. Flowers small, greenish, males in thin hanging catkins, females in small clusters at base of leaves on same twig.

Woods, lowlands and uplands, most of E US except extreme west.

Some other oaks with rounded lobed leaves — E: **Swamp White Oak; Overcup Oak; Bur Oak; English Oak;** W: **Gambel Oak** (Rockies); **Oregon White Oak** (NW); **Valley Oak** (Cal.).

Flowers spring; acorns ripen in the fall of their first year.

Fruits are acorns. Leaves leathery, distinctively lobed in the form of a cross.

A medium-sized tree with a dense crown. Flowers similar to those of other oaks. Acorns oval, brown when ripe, in deep cups covering up to a half of the acorn.

Dry ridges, floodplains; E US except far west, northeast and northwest.

Water Oak (SE US) has blue-green leaves with 3 very shallow lobes near the tip, which ends in a small bristle, and round acorns in shallow cups.

Flowers spring; acorns ripen in the fall of their second year.

Fruits are roundish, dark red-brown acorns in very shallow, stalked cups.

Large rounded spreading tree. Leaves, dull dark green above, have 7-11 shallow bristle-tipped lobes, each with a few large bristle-tipped teeth. Leaves turn red or tobacco brown in the fall. Male flowers are in reddish catkins; females dark red, in pairs.

Many habitats, also planted as a shade and street tree; most of E US except W and far S & SE; also SE Canada.

Black Oak (similar range); **California Black Oak** (valleys, SW Oregon & Calif.); **Scarlet Oak** (E US); **Pin Oak**; **Shumard Oak** (SE US); **Southern Red Oak**.

Flowers spring; acorns ripen in the fall of their second year.

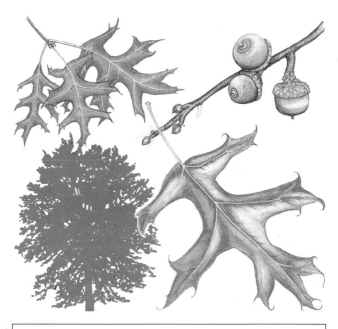

Fruits are acorns, nearly round, brown when ripe, in thin shallow cups.

Large tree with thin pin-like twigs and lower branches often sweeping the ground. Leaves, shiny dark green above, have 5-7 deep narrow lobes, each with a few bristle-tipped teeth. Leaves turn red or brown in fall. Flowers like those of Red Oak.

Wet places, uplands; CE US. Also widely planted as an ornamental.

Scarlet Oak (CE US); **Red Oak; Black Oak** (E US); **Shumard Oak** (SE US); **Jack Oak** (Lakes States); **Southern Red Oak.**

Flowers spring; acorns ripen in fall of their second year.

63

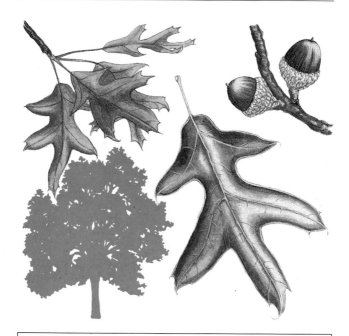

Fruits are rounded acorns, brown when ripe, in stalkless cups enclosing more than a third of the acorn.

A medium-sized rounded tree with branches often draped with "Spanish Moss." Leaves shiny green above, with 3-5 narrow lobes, each tipped with a bristle. Flowers similar to those of Red Oak and other oaks. Leaves turn brown in fall.

Uplands, mixed forest; SE US.

Pin Oak; Scarlet Oak (E US); **Black Oak** (E US); **Turkey Oak** (SSE US); **Shumard Oak** (SE US).

Flowers spring; acorns ripen in the fall of their second year.

Fruits are oval acorns, brown when ripe, in a deep, thick, short-stalked cup covered with large, loose brown scales.

Medium-sized tree. Leaves triangular, wavy-edged, with 3 broad bristle-tipped lobes towards the tip. Shiny yellow-green above, turning brown or yellow in the fall. Flowers similar to those of other oaks.

Dry uplands; SE & SNE US, except extreme west.

Water Oak; **Post Oak**.

Flowers spring; acorns ripen in the fall of their second year.

Fruits are small, brown-striped acorns in deep bowl-shaped cups, in clusters.

Small tree or shrub. Leaves dull dark green above, woolly white below, usually with 5 shallow lobes, each with one or a few bristle-tipped teeth. Leaves turn red or yellow in fall. Flowers similar to those of other oaks.

Dry and rocky ground; CNE US.

Blackjack Oak.

Flowers spring; acorns ripen in the fall of their second year.

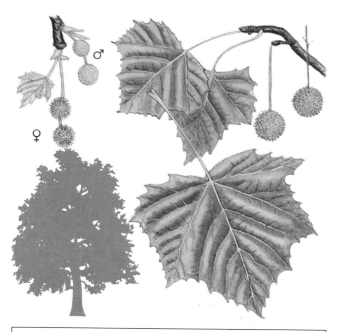

Tiny greenish flowers massed into ball-like catkins hanging on long stalks, 1 or 2 to each stalk.

Large spreading tree. Leaves with 3 or 5 shallow lobes with a few large teeth. Fruiting catkins round, brown, usually one hanging on a long stalk, with hairs on the many small nutlets.

By streams and lakes, in swamps and floodplains, mixed forests; most of E US except far north and west

London Planetree, planted as a street tree in temperate regions, has similar leaves with fewer teeth and usually 2 (or 3) round, bristly, fruiting catkins on a long stalk; **Maples: Sweetgum.**

Flowers spring; fruits in fall.

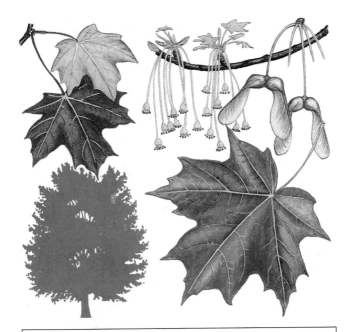

Characteristic fruits in winged pairs have pale green to brown, slightly spreading wings. All maples have these characteristic "propellers."

A large domed tree. Very thin leaves divided into 5 pointed lobes, each with a few large teeth, angles between lobes rounded. Flowers yellowish-green, in drooping clusters, appearing with the leaves. Leaves turn deep red, orange and yellow in fall.

Uplands, valleys; NE & NSE US and SE Canada.

Many types of maples grow in N America; see for example **Silver Maple** (NE US); **Japanese Maple; Fullmoon Maple; Norway Maple; Planetree Maple; Bigleaf Maple** (W).

Flowers early spring; fruits in fall.

Characteristic fruits in winged pairs, bright red wings at less than 90 degrees to each other.

Large tree with a rather narrow or rounded head. Leaves dark green above, silvery below, with 3-5 shallow, toothed, lobes. Leaf stalks red or green. Flowers reddish, in clusters wreathing the twigs before leaves appear. Spectacular red leaves in early fall.

Wet woodland, valleys, swamps, uplands, mixed broadleaf forest; most of E US (inc. Fla.) except west; also SE Canada.

Sugar Maple; Silver Maple (NE); Bigleaf Maple (W); Norway Maple; Planetree Maple; Japanese Maple; Fullmoon Maple; Sycamore; Sweetgum.

Flowers late winter; fruits spring.

Gray trunk and branches (green when young) striped with vertical pale lines.

Small tree with a short trunk. Leaves with 3 short, broad lobes towards the tip, on pinkish leaf-stalks. Flowers bright yellow, in long drooping clusters. Fruits are characteristic paired, winged nutlets.

Uplands, broadleaf forest; SE Canada and NNE US. Planted as an ornamental.

Similar oriental "snakebark" maples may be seen in parks.

Flowers late spring; fruits in fall.

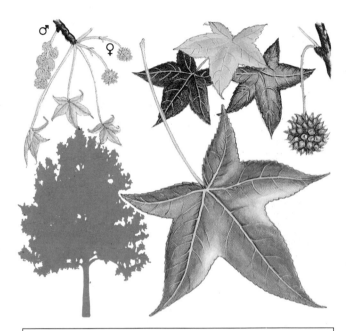

Fruits are spiky hanging balls, made up of small individual fruits, each ending in 2 prickly points.

Large conical or domed tree. Leaves star-shaped, alternate, with 3 (young trees) or 5-7 toothed lobes. Spectacular range of colors in the fall. Flowers in small green balls, male and female on the same tree.

Valleys, wet mixed woodland, often in clearings; SE (to central Florida) & SNE US. Also widely grown as an ornamental.

Planetree Maple; Sycamore.

Flowers spring; fruits in fall.

SASSAFRAS

DECIDUOUS, MEDIUM **E**

Leaves very variable in shape, always wedge-shaped at base, some unlobed, some with 2 or 3 large uneven lobes; strong scent of orange and vanilla when crushed.

Medium-sized broad-crowned tree. Leaves shiny pale green, turning red or gold in fall. Flowers yellow, in small clusters along twigs before leaves appear. Fruits are dark blue shiny berries on long red stalks.

Valleys, uplands, forest clearings; most of E US (to central Florida) except west and northwest.

None.

Flowers early spring; fruits in fall.

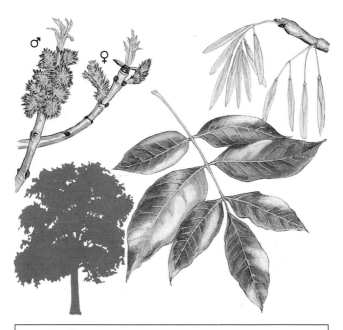

Hanging clusters of winged seeds 1¼-2¼in long, with a narrow wing. These "wings" are typical of all types of ash-tree.

A medium-sized tree with a dense rounded crown. Leaves opposite, to 10in long, usually with 7 leaflets, shiny above. Flowers without petals, in greenish clusters, appearing before the leaves. Male and female flowers on separate trees.

By streams, forests, lowlands; E US and south central Canada. Also planted for shade and shelter.

White Ash (E US); **Oregon Ash** (W US); **Velvet Ash** (SW US); Black Ash (NE US & SE Canada) has finely-toothed leaflets and purplish flowers. Other ashes occur locally.

Flowers early spring; fruits late summer to fall.

♂

Characteristic fruits in winged pairs ("propellers"), yellow with brown slightly spreading wings, in hanging strings.

Small bushy tree. Pale green leaves with 3-7 toothed leaflets which are often slightly lobed. Flowers yellow, in slender hanging bunches before leaves appear. Male and female flowers on separate trees.

By streams, valleys, roadsides; most of E US, also scattered in west and California. Also widely planted.

Green Ash; White Ash (E US); **Velvet Ash** (SW); **Oregon Ash** (W); Black Ash.

Flowers spring; fruits summer.

Large clusters of bright red berries, persisting into winter unless eaten by birds.

A small tree or shrub. Leaves have 11-17 toothed leaflets with pointed tips. Flowers with 5 separate creamy-white petals and smooth flower stalks, in large upright clusters.

Valleys and upland slopes, and in coniferous forests; NNE US & SE Canada & south in mountains. Also as an ornamental.

The very similar European Rowan is naturalized throughout N America (even Alaska); its flower stalks have fine, white hairs; Showy Mountain Ash has larger (to ½in wide) red berries.

Flowers late spring; fruits ripen in fall.

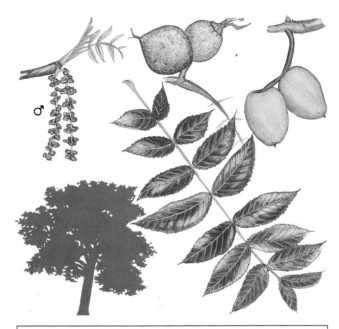

Round, warty, green fruits of Black Walnut enclose an edible nut in a thick, hard, wrinkled shell.

A large, open, rounded tree. Leaves up to 24in long with 9-21 toothed leaflets, the leaflets at the stalk end smaller than those in the middle. Male catkins green, drooping; female flowers green, at the tip of the same twig.

By streams, mixed forest; most of E US except north. Also planted.

Butternut is a medium-sized tree with similar leaves but sticky green fruits (see illustration above) are oval, enclosing a very oily nut in a thick, rough shell.

Flowers late spring, early summer; fruits in fall.

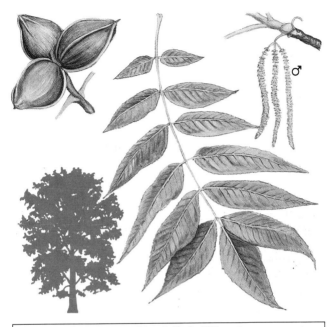

Clusters of light brown, thin-shelled edible nuts — pecans – in thin dark brown husks which split open into 4 sections when ripe.

Large domed tree. Leaves up to 20in long, made up of 11-17 opposite, toothed, leaflets. Flowers greenish, males in slender hanging catkins in clusters of 3, females in clusters of 2-10, on same twig.

Floodplains, river valleys; SE and CE US. Widely planted elsewhere for its nuts, often in plantations.

Black Walnut; Butternut; Shagbark Hickory.

Flowers early spring; fruits in fall.

77

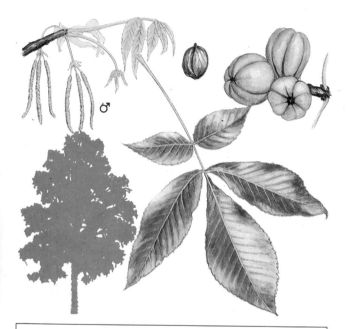

Clusters of several thin-shelled, light brown edible nuts
enclosed in thick, round, 4-lobed husks, green becoming dark
brown, splitting to base in 4 parts when ripe.

Large, narrow-headed tree with gray shaggy bark. Leaves up to
25in long with usually 5 finely-toothed leaflets. Flowers
greenish, tiny, males in clusters of 3 catkins, females in clusters of
2-5 on same twig, appearing before the leaves.

Valleys, uplands, broadleaf forest, fencerows; most of E US
except extreme S, W & NW. Cultivated for the edible nuts.

The many types of hickories are common throughout E US, with
typical 4-lobed fruits containing edible or bitter nuts. **Pecan;
Bitternut; Mockernut.**

Flowers early spring; fruits in fall.

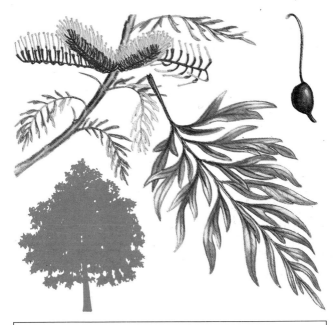

Distinctive leaves, deeply divided into narrow lobes, rolled under at the edges, shiny green above, white and silky beneath.

Medium-sized conical tree. Flowers narrow and tube-like, orange and yellow, in dense clusters along one side of the stalk. Fruits are black pods.

Planted as a street tree in Florida, S Arizona and California.

None.

Flowers spring, early summer; fruits summer, early fall.

Large hanging clusters of winged fruits, usually brown, sometimes reddish, each with a seed at the center of the twisted wing.

A medium-sized tree. Leaves up to 2 feet long with 13-41 leaflets, each one with a red stalk and 2-4 teeth near the base. Flowers unpleasantly scented, greenish, in large clusters at the ends of the shoots.

Waste places, fields, woods, as a "weed" in cities; most of temperate N America. Planted as a street tree.

None.

Flowers late spring, early summer; fruit late summer, fall.

Flowers white, sweet-scented, like sweet peas in drooping clusters.

A medium-sized tree with spiny twigs. Leaves up to 12in long, with 7-19 dark blue-green leaflets. Flat pods, dark brown when ripe, split open to release the bean-like seeds.

Native to CE US, now naturalized throughout US and S Canada, especially on rocky and sandy soils.

Honey Locust; Clammy Locust (E US & SE Canada) has pink pea-like flowers and sticky twigs; Laburnum is a small yard tree with hanging clusters of yellow pea-like flowers.

Flowers late spring; fruits in fall, remaining on tree.

81

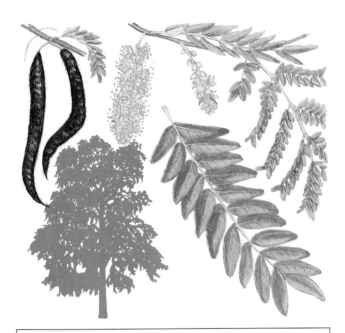

Flat, brown, hairy pods, often a foot or more long, somewhat
twisted, containing many seeds in a sweet pulp, are shed
without opening in late fall.

Large tree with an open spreading crown, and branched spines
growing from trunk and branches. Leaves, with 7-16 pairs of
leaflets, are often further divided. Flowers yellow, bell-shaped,
in small upright clusters.

Many different habitats; throughout E US except extreme west
and north. Cultivated forms often lack spines.

Black Locust; Water Locust, with similar flowers and leaves,
grows in swamps and floodplains in SE US & up the Mississippi,
and has flat, oval, papery pods.

Flowers late spring; fruits in fall.

Flowers yellow or orange, massed into small (½in diam.) sweetly scented balls along the twigs, appearing with the new leaves in late winter or early spring.

Small spiny tree or shrub. Compound leaves further subdivided, with 10-20 pairs of gray-green leaflets on each side stalk. Dark brown cylindrical pods remain on the tree throughout the winter.

Roadsides, wood edges, native to S Texas, naturalized in south from Florida to California.

Silver Wattle (S California) is an introduced tree with feathery leaves and drooping clusters of yellow fluffy balls of flowers.

Flowers late winter, early spring; fruits summer.

Round, pale brown, spiny fruits enclose 1-3 large shiny brown poisonous seeds.

A medium-sized rounded tree, the most widespread of the several native buckeyes. Leaves with 5-7 unevenly toothed leaflets all growing from the same point. Flowers yellow-green, with prominent stamens, in upright spikes.

Valleys, mountain slopes, broadleaf forest; CE US.

Horsechestnut; California Buckeye has pink and white flowers; Texas Buckeye leaves have 7-11 leaflets; Yellow Buckeye (CE US) flowers lack prominent stamens and fruits are smooth.

Flowers spring; fruits summer to fall.

Hanging clusters of many round, flat, papery fruits remain on the tree into the winter.

A small, rounded tree or shrub. Leaves with 3 leaflets all growing from the same point, on a long leafstalk. Clusters of small greenish-yellow flowers.

Dry uplands, valleys, canyons, throughout E US (including Florida) and dry SW.

None.

Flowers spring; fruits summer.

Unpleasantly scented purple flowers with 5 pale petals around a darker central tube, in long-stalked clusters.

A small tree with a dense crown. Compound leaves further subdivided into many toothed leaflets. Fruits are round yellow berries, poisonous, in clusters.

Yards, waste places, forest clearings; naturalized in SE US (including Florida) and California.

None.

Flowers spring; fruits in fall.

Large wide hanging pods, red-brown when ripe and containing several large seeds, fall unopened in winter.

Medium-sized, open-headed tree. Large leaves (to 30in long) subdivided into pairs of opposite side stalks with 6-14 oval leaflets on each stalk. Flowers greenish-white, in large upright clusters at the ends of the twigs.

Moist places, valleys, rare in wild; CE US, naturalized and planted as an ornamental further east.

Devil's Walkingstick (SE US) has similar large, subdivided leaves, but leaflets are toothed and twigs spiny.

Flowers late spring; fruits in fall.

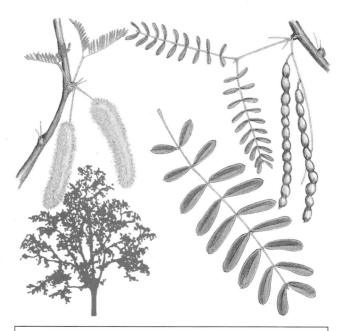

Tiny yellow flowers, sweetly-scented, in dense drooping spikes.

A small spiny tree or shrub. Paired leafstalks with 7-17 pairs of stalkless, yellow-green leaflets. Fruit is a narrow pod, constricted between each seed and filled with a sweet pulp.

Range grasslands, sandy plains, sandhills, desert and desert edges; west from Texas.

Screwbean Mesquite (SE Calif./Utah border & in Texas) has unusual spirally coiled pods; Velvet Mesquite (Arizona) is a medium-sized tree with velvety leaves, twigs and pods.

Flowers spring; fruits summer.

Leafless most of the year; leaves with 3-7 pairs of tiny
yellow-green leaflets appear in spring but soon fall.

Small spiny tree. Bark yellow-green. Flowers pale yellow, in
clusters along the bare twigs. Fruits are long, cylindrical, pointed
pods, constricted between the seeds.

Deserts, rocky foothills, mountains; Arizona, SE California.

Blue Palo Verde (along washes) has similar, brighter yellow,
flowers, but a blue-green trunk and branches.

Flowers spring; fruits summer.

89

Leaves up to 4ft in diameter, fan-shaped, divided into 50-60 stiff, pointed lobes and with leaf stalks covered with long, brown fibres.

A medium-sized tree with a crown of leaves growing from the top of the trunk, and with dead leaves partly covering the trunk. Flowers yellow, fragrant, growing in a large spike. Fruits like purple berries.

A hardy introduced tree from China, the hardiest of all palms, growing as far north as Virginia; flowering in warmer areas.

Cabbage Palmetto; Dwarf and Saw Palmettos (south) are often stemless plants, a few feet high, forming large clumps of fan-like leaves, Saw Palmetto has spiny-toothed leafstalks.

Flowers and fruits; continuous in a tropical climate.

Leaves stiff, leathery, up to 7ft in diameter, fan-shaped, deeply divided into many narrow segments; leafstalks without spines.

Medium-sized tree with a crown of drooping leaves. Upper part of trunk covered in old leaf bases. Flowers white, sweetly-scented, in drooping spikes. Fruits are shiny black berries.

Native to Florida, planted widely in the south.

California Fan Palm; Cabbage Palm; Chusan Palm.

Flowers early summer; fruits in fall.

CABBAGE PALM
EVERGREEN/MEDIUM **E & W**

Leaves thin, soft, up to 8ft wide, fan-shaped, deeply divided into around 70 narrow segments, with divided, drooping tips. Leafstalks with spines on young trees.

Tall tree with a gray trunk, free of leaf bases on older trees, and with a crown of arching and drooping foliage. Fragrant, creamy yellow flowers in large spikes. Fruits are purple-black berries with a white waxy bloom.

Introduced from Australia, grown as a street and ornamental tree in California and the drier parts of the south.

Chinese Fan Palm is a similar, smaller tree with less deeply divided leaves and bluish-white berries.

Flowers and fruit; produced continuously in tropical climates.

CALIFORNIA FAN PALM ☀

W (& E) EVERGREEN, MEDIUM

Leaves up to 5 feet in diameter, fan-shaped, divided into many narrow, pointed segments; leaf-stalks have hooked spines.

Medium-sized evergreen tree with a skirt of dead leaves hanging around the trunk. Flowers white, funnel-shaped, in drooping clusters. Fruits are black berries.

Native S. California desert, widely planted elsewhere in south as a street tree.

Cabbage Palmetto; Chusan Palm.

Flowers and fruits; continuous in tropical climates.

Leaves up to 15ft long (on 3ft leafstalks), with many narrow, pointed leaflets, up to 3ft long, at different angles to the main stalk, giving the crown a plumy appearance.

A medium-sized tree with a tall, smooth, ringed, gray trunk and a crown of arching or drooping foliage. Flowers yellow, in sprays up to 6ft long, arising among the leaves, drooping as the large bunches of yellow and brown fruits develop.

Introduced as a street and ornamental tree in Florida and southern California.

Royalpalm is a taller tree with the trunk swollen in the middle, hardy only in southern Florida; Kingpalm (Calif. & Fla.) has leaves with flat rows of leaflets, flowers arise below leaves.

Flowers and fruits; continuous in tropical climates.

Leaves up to 20in long, divided into many narrow leaflets and with spiny leafstalks.

Medium-sized tree with a massive trunk covered with old leaf bases. Small white flowers in large clusters develop into large bunches of yellow, rather tasteless, dates.

Hot, dry climates, introduced across US in the south.

The true Date Palm has more tasty fruit and is cultivated in California.

Flowers and fruit; continuous in tropical climates.

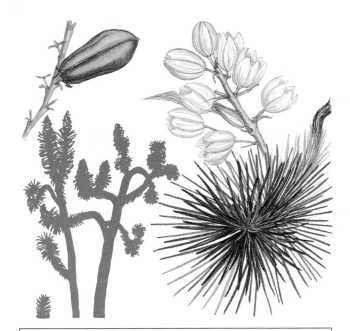

Grotesque small tree of the Mojave Desert, with stiff sharp narrow leaves clustered at the ends of the branches.

Flowers greenish-yellow, bell-shaped, unpleasantly scented, in large upright clusters at the ends of the branches. Fruit is a large green or brown pod.

Joshua tree is the largest of the many yuccas common in hot dry regions across the south.

Other common yuccas that grow to "tree size" are Aloe Yucca (S US), leaves edged with tiny teeth, flowers white; Soaptree Yucca (SW), gray-green untoothed leaves, white flowers.

Flowers early spring; fruit falls from the tree in late spring.

96

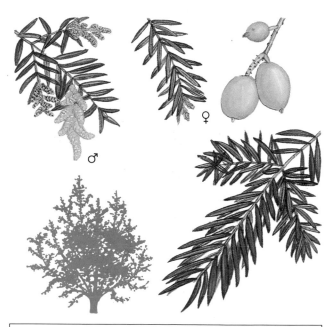

Fruits are round, green ripening to yellow; with sweet flesh enclosing a hard stone.

A medium-sized spreading tree. Narrow, pointed leaves with 2 bluish bands underneath are set all round the twig. Male flowers yellow, in narrow clusters, females green, on separate trees.

Planted as an ornamental in SW US.

English Yew.

Flowers early summer; fruits in fall.

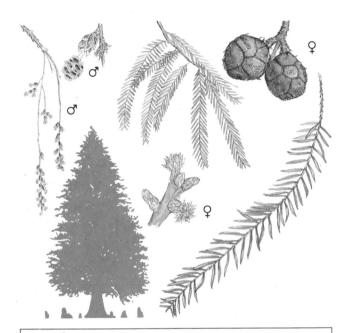

Leaves flat, soft, delicate, ½in long, a bright light green when young, darker later, set alternately on side shoots which are shed complete with the leaves in fall.

Large conical tree with a domed top. Roots form "knees" above ground in wet soil or when growing in water. Male flowers in catkins 4in long, female cones small, round, bright green at first, later purplish, often on separate trees.

Swamps, floodplains, often in water; SSE US (to central Florida). Widely grown elsewhere on drier ground.

Coast Redwood.

Flowering cones: most noticeable in spring.

Leaves hard, dark green, flat, ½-¾in long, with sharp points and 2 white bands underneath, arranged in 2 rows on either side of the shoot; older shoots covered in scale-like leaves.

Very tall columnar tree often becoming thin with age. Very thick soft stringy reddish bark. Yellow male flowers at end of young shoots, female cones small, round, with wrinkled scales.

Native to coastal belt from S Oregon to California. Widely planted elsewhere.

Baldcypress.

Flowering cones: early spring.

Leaves soft, flat, 3/8-5/8in long, with rounded tips, shiny dark green above, 2 white bands below, in 2 rows each side of the shoot with an extra row along top of shoot, white sides up.

Medium to large pyramidal tree with a drooping leading tip. Twigs have peglike leaf bases. Male flowers bright yellow, in clustered cones on the undersides of the twigs, female cones green at first, then brown, hanging singly at the ends of the twigs.

Upland valleys and slopes; NE US and NSE US in mountains. Also grown as an ornamental.

Western Hemlock (Pacific Northwest); **Douglas Fir.**

Flowering cones: spring.

Leaves soft, flattened, ¾-1½in long, dark yellow-green or blue-green above with 2 whitish bands below; spreading in 2 complex rows along each side of the shoots.

A very tall narrow tree with a pointed top. Male flowers yellow, on underside of shoots, towards the tip. Female cones drooping, green at first, brown when ripe. 2-3½in long, with prominent spiky brown bracts.

NW US & SW Canada, south in Rockies (Rocky Mountain Douglas Fir, a smaller tree) and along the coast. Also planted.

Giant Fir; Noble Fir; Red Fir; Western Hemlock; Eastern Hemlock.

Flowering cones: spring.

Leaves ⅝-1⅜in long, leathery, strongly curved, blue-green on both sides, curving around the branches from below, in 4 rows.

A very tall conical tree. Leaves leave flat round scars on twigs when they fall off. Female cones erect, yellowish at first, purple-brown with green bracts when mature, up to 10in long, breaking up on tree to release seeds.

Mountains in NW US. Planted elsewhere.

Red Fir; Balsam Fir; Giant Fir; Douglas Fir.

Flowering cones: spring.

♀

Leaves slender, soft, dark or blue-green with whitish lines, pointing out all round twig except along underside.

Tall narrow conical tree with flaky gray and orange bark. Male flowers dark purple, females reddish-purple, developing into shiny light brown cones (to 2½in long) hanging at the ends of twigs. Peg-like projections on twigs where leaves have fallen.

SW Canada southwards in Rocky Mountains. Cultivated varieties with paler blue-green foliage are also grown.

Blue Spruce; White & Black Spruces (Canada & NE US); **Red Spruce; Norway Spruce;** Sitka Spruce is a very tall tree from the NW coast (Alaska to N Calif.) with very spiny foliage.

Flowering cones: spring.

Leaves short, stout, curved, bright shiny green with whitish lines, sharp and wiry, pointing out all around the twig.

Large conical tree. Male flowers crimson, females purplish, developing into hanging reddish-brown cones (to 1½in long) with stiff scales. Small peg-like projections left on twigs where leaves have been shed (as in all spruces).

Rocky soils in mountains; NE US & SE Canada, and south in mountains.

Black Spruce & White Spruce (Canada & NE US); **Engelmann Spruce; Norway Spruce; Blue Spruce.**

Flowering cones: spring.

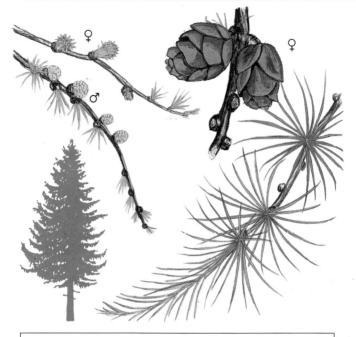

Leaves soft, slender, ¾-1in long, bright green, in clusters of around 30 along the twigs; leaves turn yellow before they are shed in fall.

A medium to large, thin-crowned, pyramidal tree. Male flowers yellow, females red, developing into small (¾in long) egg-shaped cones made up of a few scales, brown when mature, upright on the twig.

Uplands, bogs, swamps; Canada (to Alaska) and NE US. Also planted as an ornamental.

Western Larch (mts. SW Can. & NW US) is a very narrow tall tree whose cones have the bracts protruding between the scales; European Larch has larger cones (1-1¼in long).

Flowering cones: early spring.

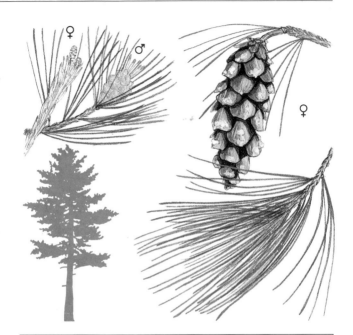

Pines differ from other conifers in their needles, set in sheathed bundles of 2, 3 or 5. White Pine has fine, blue-green needles, 2½-5in long, in 5's, growing densely on the branches.

Tall tree with a straight, gray-brown trunk and horizontal branches. Male flowers whitish tipped with pink, on new shoots, female cones narrow, pointed, 4-8in long, with thin rounded spreading scales when mature.

Widespread in NE US and SE Can. The other types of 5-needle pines occur in mts. in W North America (e.g. **Sugar Pine**).

Some other pines in NE America: **Scotch Pine** (also planted on W coast); **Austrian Pine**; Red Pine — long needles in pairs, snap cleanly when bent; reddish trunk. **Pitch Pine.**

Flowering cones: early summer.

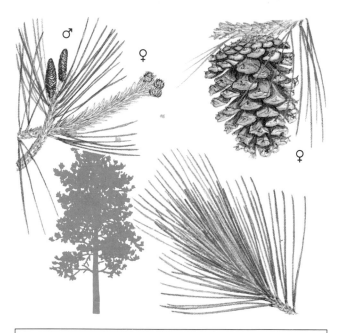

Stout, curved, dark green needles in bundles of 2 or 3, 4-8in long, set in dense tufts (at the ends of the branches on older trees).

Often very large tree with a broad conical crown. Mature female cones egg-shaped, 2-6in long, dark brown with thick scales, each bearing a small sharp curved prickle. Bark pink-brown, split into large flat plates on older trees.

Forests, usually in mountains, throughout west. Many other types of 3-needle pines grow in N America.

See other **Pines.**

Flowering cones: spring.

Very long (10-15in) dark green needles in bundles of 3, set densely on the branches.

A tall tree with an open crown, twigs ending in a large white bud. Dull brown female cones 6-10in long, opening when ripe, each blunt-ended scale ending in a small prickle. Male flowers clustered in a narrow head at tip of shoot.

Foothills, lowlands, sandhills, along coast; Coastal Plain of SE US.

Some other southeastern pines: **Shortleaf Pine** (2-3 needles), **Slash Pine** (2-3), **Loblolly Pine** (3).

Flowering cones: spring.

Stout, light green needles, ¾-1½in long, in pairs.

A small bushy tree. Male flowers yellow in large cluster. Female cones egg-shaped. 1½-2in long, yellow-brown and sticky, opening to release the large, edible seeds.

Dry rocky places, open woods, foothills; SW US.

Several other varieties of Pinyon Pine occur in the southwest, with needles in 3's or, more rarely, singly.

Flowering cones: late spring.

Variety illustrated is Utah Juniper.

Fruit is a berry, most commonly blue with a whitish bloom, and containing one or several seeds.

Small spreading trees or shrubs. Twigs covered with pointed scale-like leaves, usually opposite, in 4 rows. Young trees also have prickly needle-like leaves. Male flowers yellow, at the tips of the shoots.

Dry rocky soils, often in mountains; throughout western US.

Many junipers are grown as ornamental shrubs or small trees.

Flowering cones: early spring; fruits (female cones) fall.

Fruits are soft, juicy, dark blue berries with a white bloom, containing one or two seeds.

A medium-sized columnar tree. Slender twigs covered with aromatic dark green, scale-like leaves, opposite, in 4 rows; needle-like leaves also present. Male flowers yellow.

Uplands, old farmland, fencerows; most of E US. Also cultivated as an ornamental.

Western Junipers.

Flowering cones early spring; fruits in fall.

Foliage in sprays of small, hard, dark green or gray pointed scales, smelling of aniseed when crushed.

Very tall tree with a distinctive pointed crown. Very thick, resilient, stringy pinkish brown bark. Male flowers yellow, at ends of shoots. Female cones on long stalks in ones and twos, about 3¼in long.

Isolated groves in the Sierra Nevada in California. Planted elsewhere.

None.

Flowering cones: late fall to spring.

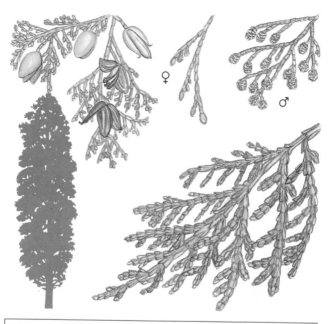

Distinctive cones composed of 6 flattened cone scales, yellow-green turning brown when mature.

Large tree with a columnar crown. Flat, branched twigs made up of shiny green, aromatic, overlapping scale-like leaves, opposite, in 4 rows. Male flowers numerous, often coloring tree yellow.

Mountains, mixed coniferous forest; NW US and south in mountains to S California. Also grown as an ornamental.

Western Red Cedar.

Flowering cones: late winter, early spring.

Female cones numerous, urn-shaped, about ½in long, leathery, green at first, later brown, only central 6 scales bear seeds, 2-3 on each scale.

Very large tree. Much branched twigs in horizontal flattened sprays, composed of shiny dark green, aromatic, scale-like leaves. Male flowers dark red, at tips of twigs.

Extensive forests in NW US & SW Canada, south along coast and in northern Rockies.

Oriental Arborvitae (with similar leaves) is a small tree widely grown as an ornamental in warm temperate regions; **Incense Cedar; Northern White Cedar.**

Flowering cones: spring.

114

Female cones tiny (¼in diameter), round, bluish becoming brown when ripe, all 6 cone scales bearing 1 or 2 seeds.

A large tree with a conical crown. Slender twigs branched in several planes, made up of dull blue-green scale-like leaves, opposite. Male flowers reddish, at tips of twigs.

Swamps; Atlantic Coast south from Maine to N Florida and coastal belt west to Mississippi. Also grown as an ornamental.

Sawara Falsecypress; Monterey Cypress; Port-Orford-Cedar (with a limited range in the wild in the NW, but cultivated in NW) has similar cones with 8 scales.

Flowering cones: early spring.

Many small (½in diameter), round cones, green at first, becoming brown, with 10 pointed scales.

Large narrow pyramidal tree. Foliage made up of horizontally flattened sprays of branched twigs, composed of blue-green, pointed scale-like leaves, opposite, in 4 rows. Underside of foliage whitish. Male flowers pale brown at tips of twigs.

Many varieties cultivated as ornamentals, with drooping, yellow or very slender twigs.

Northern White Cedar; Monterey Cypress; Port-Orford-Cedar (grown in NW) has similar cones with 8 scales.

Flowering cones: spring.

116

Many large lumpy cones (around 1½ in diameter), green at first, later shiny brown, with 8-12 rounded scales, remaining closed when mature.

Medium-sized tree with a flattened crown in exposed positions on coast, taller and narrower in cultivation. Bright green foliage is irregularly branched. Male flowers, at tips of shoots behind female cones.

Rare in the wild on the Californian coast; widely planted for shelter and as an ornamental along Pacific Coast.

Arizona Cypress (rare in wild in SW) has similar cones and dull gray-green foliage, and is also in cultivation.

Flowering cones: early spring.

Lookalikes & Other Species

Shingle Oak (1) Leaves shiny dark green above, hairy below.
Laurel Oak (2) Nearly evergreen leaves shiny above, slightly shiny below.
California Live Oak (3) Evergreen leaves edged with small spiny teeth. **Canyon Live Oak** (4) Large round acorns in golden hairy cups. **Chinkapin Oak** (5) Brown striped acorns in deep, thin, gray cups.
Swamp Chestnut Oak (6) Wide, chestnut-like leaves, acorns in deep thick cups.
Swamp White Oak (7) Acorns in deep cups, leaves with 5-10 pairs of shallow lobes.
Overcup Oak (8) Round acorns almost enclosed by the cup. **Bur Oak** (9) Acorns in deep cups with fringed edges, very large leaves. **Gambel Oak** (10) Shiny dark green leaves with 7-11 deep lobes.

Lookalikes & Other Species

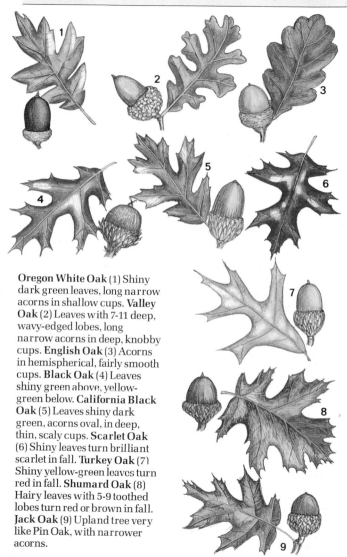

Oregon White Oak (1) Shiny dark green leaves, long narrow acorns in shallow cups. **Valley Oak** (2) Leaves with 7-11 deep, wavy-edged lobes, long narrow acorns in deep, knobby cups. **English Oak** (3) Acorns in hemispherical, fairly smooth cups. **Black Oak** (4) Leaves shiny green above, yellow-green below. **California Black Oak** (5) Leaves shiny dark green, acorns oval, in deep, thin, scaly cups. **Scarlet Oak** (6) Shiny leaves turn brilliant scarlet in fall. **Turkey Oak** (7) Shiny yellow-green leaves turn red in fall. **Shumard Oak** (8) Hairy leaves with 5-9 toothed lobes turn red or brown in fall. **Jack Oak** (9) Upland tree very like Pin Oak, with narrower acorns.

Lookalikes & Other Species

Pacific Dogwood (1) The "flowers," 4-6in across, usually have 6 bracts. **Sweetbay** (2) Small deciduous tree with white flowers. **Bigleaf Magnolia** (3) Deciduous leaves are up to 30in long. **Cucumber Tree** (4) Greenish-yellow bell-shaped flowers.
Rhododendron (5) Showy lilac-purple flowers in clusters (also other colors). **Camellia** (6) Evergreen shrub or small tree with red, pink or white flowers. **Red Iron-bark Eucalyptus** (7) Red-barked tree with short, broad, pointed leaves. **Paulownia** (8) Large-leaved tree with spikes of purple flowers. **White Willow** (9) Leaves whitish and silky below; naturalized near cities. **Sugarberry** (10) Curved leaves often untoothed.

Lookalikes & Other Species

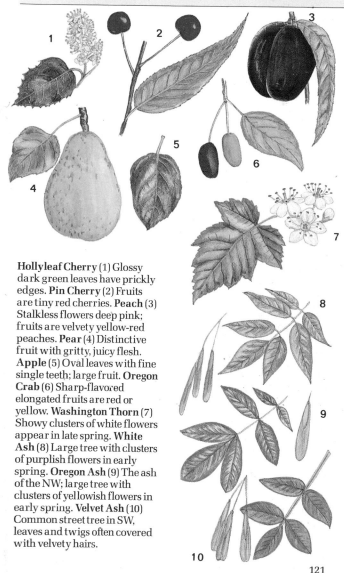

Hollyleaf Cherry (1) Glossy dark green leaves have prickly edges. **Pin Cherry** (2) Fruits are tiny red cherries. **Peach** (3) Stalkless flowers deep pink; fruits are velvety yellow-red peaches. **Pear** (4) Distinctive fruit with gritty, juicy flesh. **Apple** (5) Oval leaves with fine single teeth; large fruit. **Oregon Crab** (6) Sharp-flavored elongated fruits are red or yellow. **Washington Thorn** (7) Showy clusters of white flowers appear in late spring. **White Ash** (8) Large tree with clusters of purplish flowers in early spring. **Oregon Ash** (9) The ash of the NW; large tree with clusters of yellowish flowers in early spring. **Velvet Ash** (10) Common street tree in SW, leaves and twigs often covered with velvety hairs.

Lookalikes & Other Species

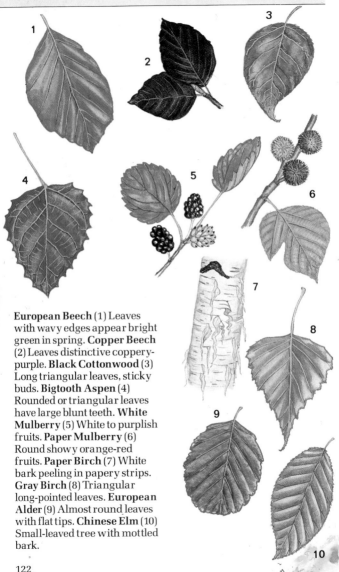

European Beech (1) Leaves with wavy edges appear bright green in spring. **Copper Beech** (2) Leaves distinctive coppery-purple. **Black Cottonwood** (3) Long triangular leaves, sticky buds. **Bigtooth Aspen** (4) Rounded or triangular leaves have large blunt teeth. **White Mulberry** (5) White to purplish fruits. **Paper Mulberry** (6) Round showy orange-red fruits. **Paper Birch** (7) White bark peeling in papery strips. **Gray Birch** (8) Triangular long-pointed leaves. **European Alder** (9) Almost round leaves with flat tips. **Chinese Elm** (10) Small-leaved tree with mottled bark.

Lookalikes & Other Species

Silver Maple (1) Leaves with 5 deep lobes are silvery below. **Japanese Maple** (2) Leaves with 7-11 pointed lobes; a small yard tree. **Fullmoon Maple** (3) Round leaves with 7-11 pointed lobes; small yard tree. **Norway Maple** (4) Winged fruits have wings curving away from each other. **Planetree Maple** (5) Leaves have 5 pointed toothed lobes. **Bigleaf Maple** (6) The maple of the NW; very large leaves, 6-12in across. **Chinkapins** (7) Small trees with spiny burs enclosing a single shiny brown nut. **Bitternut** (8) Bright yellow buds most noticeable in winter. **Mockernut** (9) Edible nuts in thick shells enclosed in thick husks. **Horsechestnut** (10) White or pink flowers in showy spikes.

Lookalikes & Other Species

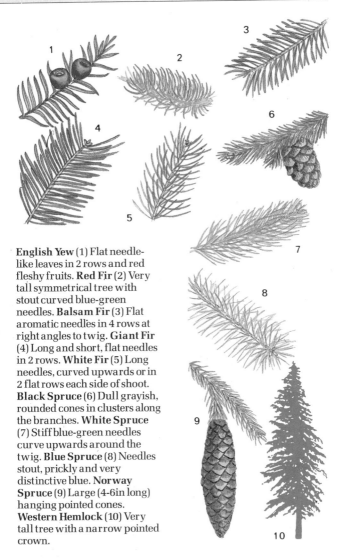

English Yew (1) Flat needle-like leaves in 2 rows and red fleshy fruits. **Red Fir** (2) Very tall symmetrical tree with stout curved blue-green needles. **Balsam Fir** (3) Flat aromatic needles in 4 rows at right angles to twig. **Giant Fir** (4) Long and short, flat needles in 2 rows. **White Fir** (5) Long needles, curved upwards or in 2 flat rows each side of shoot. **Black Spruce** (6) Dull grayish, rounded cones in clusters along the branches. **White Spruce** (7) Stiff blue-green needles curve upwards around the twig. **Blue Spruce** (8) Needles stout, prickly and very distinctive blue. **Norway Spruce** (9) Large (4-6in long) hanging pointed cones. **Western Hemlock** (10) Very tall tree with a narrow pointed crown.

Lookalikes & Other Species

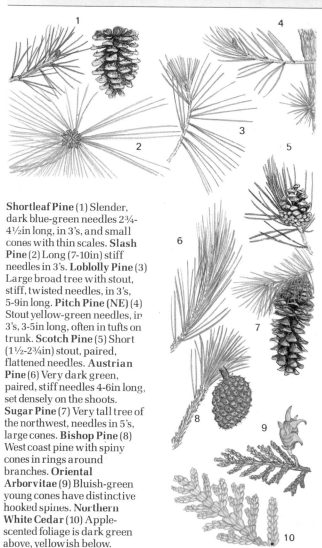

Shortleaf Pine (1) Slender, dark blue-green needles 2¾-4½in long, in 3's, and small cones with thin scales. **Slash Pine** (2) Long (7-10in) stiff needles in 3's. **Loblolly Pine** (3) Large broad tree with stout, stiff, twisted needles, in 3's, 5-9in long. **Pitch Pine** (NE) (4) Stout yellow-green needles, in 3's, 3-5in long, often in tufts on trunk. **Scotch Pine** (5) Short (1½-2¾in) stout, paired, flattened needles. **Austrian Pine** (6) Very dark green, paired, stiff needles 4-6in long, set densely on the shoots. **Sugar Pine** (7) Very tall tree of the northwest, needles in 5's, large cones. **Bishop Pine** (8) West coast pine with spiny cones in rings around branches. **Oriental Arborvitae** (9) Bluish-green young cones have distinctive hooked spines. **Northern White Cedar** (10) Apple-scented foliage is dark green above, yellowish below.

Index and Check-list

All species in roman type are illustrated.

Keep a record of your sightings by checking the boxes.